The
Curiosity Cabinet

IAN WALLACE

GROUNDWOOD BOOKS
HOUSE OF ANANSI PRESS
TORONTO BERKELEY

Text and illustrations copyright © 2017 by Ian Wallace
Published in Canada and the USA in 2017 by Groundwood Books

All rights reserved. No part of this publication may be reproduced, stored in a retrieval system or transmitted,
in any form or by any means, without the prior written consent of the publisher or a license from The Canadian
Copyright Licensing Agency (Access Copyright). For an Access Copyright license, visit www.accesscopyright.ca
or call toll free to 1-800-893-5777.

Groundwood Books / House of Anansi Press
groundwoodbooks.com

We acknowledge for their financial support of our publishing program the Canada Council for the Arts, the
Ontario Arts Council and the Government of Canada.

Library and Archives Canada Cataloguing in Publication
Wallace, Ian, author
The curiosity cabinet / Ian Wallace.
Issued in print and electronic formats.
ISBN 978-1-55498-922-5 (hardcover).—ISBN 978-1-55498-923-2 (PDF)
1. Wallace, Ian—Juvenile literature. 2. Authors, Canadian—
Biography — Pictorial works — Juvenile literature. 3. Wallace, Ian —
Travel — Juvenile literature. I. Title.
PS8595.A566Z46 2017   jC813'.54   C2016-908191-5
C2016-908192-3

Design by Michael Solomon
Printed and bound in Malaysia

Contents

—

Introduction

In my home stands a tall, finely crafted cabinet of curiosities. Its contents represent the four decades I have traveled Canada from sea to sea to sea, telling stories in words and pictures.

On those journeys, I flew over jagged Rocky Mountain peaks; criss-crossed golden prairies; traversed frozen tundra, boreal forests, pristine lakes and rivers; and swept over glistening icebergs. I visited cities and towns, villages and outports with arresting names like Come By Chance, Sheshatshit, Moose Jaw and Zeballos.

When not telling stories, I went salmon fishing off Vancouver Island and dogsledding with world-champion musher Eddy Streeper in northern British Columbia.

I was taken on a caribou hunt with Dene hunters in the Northwest Territories and stood on the Arctic Circle when the temperature hovered at -48 degrees Celsius (-54 degrees Fahrenheit).

On the shore of Pipestone Creek in northern Alberta, I encountered a cliff that held dinosaur bones, most likely of the *Pachyrhinosaurus*, in strata of dark sediment.

One November night I witnessed a rare sight, a solely red aurora borealis dancing in a wintery Whitehorse sky.

I ate things I'd never eaten before. Bannock and Arctic char, seal flipper pie and cod tongues, bear, elk, caribou and moose.

I met children, teens and adults from every walk of life, ethnicity and faith, and made new friends across the country.

One day I realized that this vast land was a nation of families and diverse neighborhoods, and that I had left a piece of myself in each one —

and they in me. Always, I was welcomed with kindness, generous hospitality and good humor.

As the decades passed, the number of kilometers I traveled clicked into the tens of thousands, the number of provinces and territories climbed, the number of young people I read to approached one million and counting, causing a close friend to nickname me "Captain Canada."

Often, teachers and librarians shared intimate stories of the impact my books had had on their students and readers. In elementary schools, my stories enabled two sensitive young girls, both select mutes, to speak for the first time in several years. One university student told me how my author/illustrator visit had impacted him so profoundly that he decided that day to become an artist. Each story left me deeply touched and gratified.

I was given countless thanks-for-coming gifts: mugs, thermoses, pens, T-shirts, handwritten notes and notepads, student writing and art, and occasionally, something handcrafted by a town artisan to remind me of the community.

In one Winnipeg elementary school I found the greatest gift of my life — a teacher/librarian who became my wife.

Each of these gifts and experiences has become part of my curiosity cabinet. Most are not priceless treasures to anyone but me, yet they remind me of the extraordinary adventures I have had and the people who have enriched my life all across this land. As a child, I never could have imagined the wondrous life I would lead.

Come and take a look inside.

ONTARIO

present

Alistair
MacLeod

The Lost Salt
Gift of Blood

to Ian Wallace from Barton School - 1996

Scotia

ova

15

NEW BRUNSWICK

These earrings were made especially for your wife by my niece Arlene Diabo.

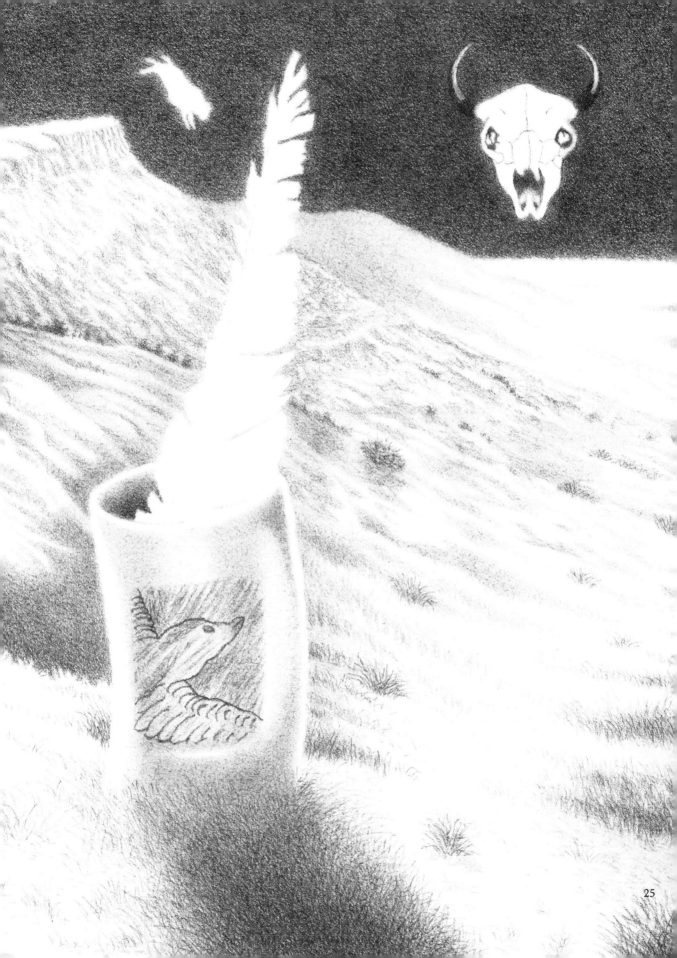

25

PRINCE ALBE
CRIMP CUT
LONG BURNING PIPE AN
CIGARETTE TOBACCO

Illustrator's Notes

In August 2014, my editor, Sheila Barry, asked me if I'd consider creating a book for the 150th anniversary of Canada's Confederation. Shortly thereafter, my wife, Deb, suggested a curiosity cabinet of iconic Canadian things. Her suggestion came a year after she and I had visited the Pitt Rivers and Ashmolean museums in Oxford, England, where we saw galleries displaying curiosity cabinets chock-full of glorious and bizarre antiquities from around the globe.

The objects in my cabinet are comprised of gifts I've been given, experiences I've had or purchases I've made while visiting communities nationwide, each and every one having left an indelible impression.

COVER

The cabinet's wooden doors open, several Canadian coins tumble out, and a Yukon raven perched on a Vancouver Island Douglas-fir root beckons the reader to look inside.

FRONT ENDPAPER

Using pencils ranging from 7A, the softest and faintest, to 8B, the hardest and darkest, on Arches watercolor paper, I have drawn just a small sampling of the gifts I've received from young readers. They remind me why I've loved making author/illustrator visits and why I still do them today. There are few things that bring me as much fulfillment as inspiring kids through books.

HALF-TITLE PAGE

When I was a boy growing up in Niagara Falls in the 1950s, a map of Canada hung in every classroom of my elementary school. I often fantasized that some day I'd travel to every province and territory. The snow globe illuminates the moment I stood on the Arctic Circle, which is about as far as I could go from my childhood home and still be in the country.

DEDICATION AND TITLE PAGES

Red Converse All Stars and zany socks became my signature look in the 1980s, so it is appropriate that one or the other appears as the cabinet doors open to reveal the contents inside.

ONTARIO

Leaping back in time, I begin with my home province where my desire to be an artist and writer was born and nurtured.

Inside this second snow globe is an image based on a photograph circa 1978, taken during a reading of *The Sandwich* at the Owen Sound Public Library. In the original photo the children's librarian can be seen making mortadella and provolone sandwiches, which we served later that afternoon to all intrepid eaters.

The delicately carved sparrow perched on a chunk of grape vine was a gift from the Niagara Falls Public Library on the launch of my sixth book, *The Sparrow's Song*, set in the cataract city. It was given to me by Miss Albrant, the children's librarian who inspired me with my earliest library books decades before.

I received the family of tamarack geese during visits to Attawapiskat and Moose Factory. Two decades later the scent of tamarack still permeates the birds and can thrust me back to those fall days spent on frozen James Bay. Historically, life-size models of these geese were made by Cree hunters to be used as decoys during the spring and fall hunting seasons. Today, smaller versions are made as gifts or souvenirs.

NEWFOUNDLAND AND LABRADOR

Between 1986 and 2006, I visited "The Rock" so frequently that this mainlander from Upper Canada was made an honorary Newfoundlander — being "screeched in" by kissing a cod and tossing back a glass of "screech" (rum) to make it official.

Lurking about the stark wood sculpture of a fishing-stage façade stand two outrageously dressed mummers, one mimicking a hobbyhorse, gifts from Newfoundland friends upon the publication of *The Mummer's Song*. The two outporters celebrate the Celtic tradition of house visiting during the Twelve Days of Christmas when evenings of boisterous partying ensue.

On the right is an Innu Tea Doll purchased for Deb in Sheshatshit, Labrador. (The town sign was stolen so frequently that the spelling has since been changed to Sheshatshiu.) Traditionally, dolls of both sexes were given to young family members to teach a sense of responsibility. The child's task was to carry the handmade doll, packed tightly with one kilogram (two pounds) of tea, from one hunting ground to the next. When tea was needed, especially for hunters and elders, the back of the doll was opened and the tea extracted. Only after all the tea was consumed could the doll be stuffed with grass or leaves and become a cherished companion.

PRINCE EDWARD ISLAND

I've celebrated PEI with a banner that riffs on the provincial flag and hung it from a rod with lobster-buoy finials. The English heraldic lion exclaims, "Whoa … what a bargain!" over a heaping bucket of mussels priced at a mere $2.99 in 1988.

In the moonlit Gulf of St. Lawrence, a pair of lips forms both an island and a kiss, inspired by the lithograph *O Canada*, created by the late artist, Joyce Wieland.

NOVA SCOTIA

On a large scallop shell, maritime artist Marion Duncan painted this striking image that speaks proudly of a stalwart people, while lauding their history with the sea. The lobster stand is my concoction.

Illuminating this tableau is a miner's lamp, a gift from my mother, in memory of my grandfather who was a child miner and the inspiration for my book *Boy of the Deeps*. At the same time, I am honoring the importance of research in the lives of authors and illustrators — the need to stand squarely on the earth where a story is set, smell the air and walk among the people who inhabit the landscape. In the research phase for *Boy of the Deeps*, I not only unearthed invaluable information about coal mining in Cape Breton, but I stumbled upon the work of one of Canada's finest novelists, Alistair MacLeod — a golden revelation.

NEW BRUNSWICK

The first time I saw whales cavorting in the Bay of Fundy, I marveled at their magnificence while feeling extraordinarily small. In their presence, I was forced to confront the fragility of their existence in the natural world today and why they need protecting.

Below the cabinet shelf and ocean's surface, the tragic history of whaling is illustrated through scrimshaw — carvings once done on whale teeth and bone — including the loss of human life that frequently occurred during an arduous hunt.

QUEBEC

In this still life, *la belle province* is represented by the curiosity cabinet itself, which holds the mementoes from forty years of travel. The cabinet is styled after one I purchased in Old Montreal, crafted by two Québécois furniture makers who employed the nineteenth-century tools that had belonged to their great-grandfathers. No nails were used in the cabinet's construction, only wood pegs. The fleurs-de-lis were carved by hand.

In addition, there are two considerate gifts from Kateri School on the Kahnawake Reserve — one for me, the other for Deb.

MANITOBA

Of all the gifts I have been given, the most cherished one danced out of the prairie wearing a red dress — Deb. This image honors her professional life in 1985 as a teacher/librarian as well as the beginnings of our relationship. Dominating the bulletin board is a robust rooster crowing in a new day in our lives and a kiss of abiding affection. Beneath a changing sky and a prairie storm are Nelda's sticky buns, which we noshed on whenever I went to Winnipeg. An ode to young love and the most delicious sticky buns in Canada. When I drew the pastries on the shelf, they reminded me of wheat bales on the bald prairie.

SASKATCHEWAN

A cabinet shelf echoes the flat Saskatchewan landscape under a big prairie sky. "Lucky Money" is falling from red packets traditionally given to children during Chinese New Year celebrations. I was often the beneficiary of these packets in recognition of my book *Chin Chiang and the Dragon's Dance*. This drawing incorporates an important juncture in Chinese Canadian history — an 1858 coin acknowledges the year significant numbers of Chinese migrants arrived in British Columbia during Canada's Gold Rush. Other coins representing Canada's history include an early coin from France, circa 1635; the heads of two queens (Victoria and Elizabeth II) and a king (George V); one from World War II; 1967 Centennial coins; and the iconic *Bluenose* schooner, beaver and moose, loonie and toonie.

ALBERTA

At Head-Smashed-In Buffalo Jump, the wind always blows, the Rocky Mountains rise to the west, and the prairie spreads from the cliff's base as far as the eye can see. Archeological evidence gathered from this bison kill site dates back nearly six thousand years. It is one of the most starkly beautiful, soul-inspiring places I have ever visited.

The eagle feather in the white porcelain vase respects this site as native land. The vase itself, with a young sparrow drawn into the porcelain, was crafted by Brynn in 3B at Calgary Jewish School. Her drawing represents her favorite of my books, *The Sparrow's Song*.

BRITISH COLUMBIA

In the forest of Cathedral Grove on Vancouver Island, giant Douglas-fir trees, the largest eight hundred years old, sink their roots into the fertile earth and poke their spires into the distant sky. Amazingly, some of these trees have a girth of 9 meters (29 feet) and grow as tall as 75 meters (250 feet). Sheltered inside one of the ancient trees, I was overwhelmed by nature's grandeur and hummed, "O Canada …"

YUKON

As a boy, I dreamed of visiting the Land of the Midnight Sun to experience the aurora borealis and the place that begat the larger-than-life characters Sam McGee and Dan McGrew, created by the Yukon writer Robert Service.

In 1982, my childhood's wildest expectations were fulfilled. I visited the Sourdough Saloon in Dawson City, home of the Sourtoe Cocktail, its infamous ingredient stored inside a Prince Albert tobacco tin. Equally enthralling was an evening with the artist and witty raconteur Ted Harrison, whose paintings I had admired but whose color work I didn't fully comprehend until I traveled north of 60. There I discovered that the quality of light is distinctly different than in southern Ontario. To Ted and that trip I owe an enormous debt of gratitude because they brought into my mind's eye the colors critical to the visual interpretation of Jan Andrews' story *Very Last First Time*.

Classic details of northern life found in Ted's paintings float across the undulating night sky.

NORTHWEST TERRITORIES/NUNAVUT

During a visit to Spence Bay in 1986, in what was then the Northwest Territories (now Taloyoak, Nunavut), I met Inuit carvers working in their homes. In one, a piece of soapstone was being carved on a kitchen countertop, the body of a polar bear just beginning to emerge, and alongside it a frozen slab of caribou meat was defrosting. Blood seeping from the meat pooled across the counter and dripped onto the floor. In that singular moment, life and art merged and became inseparable.

A decade later, I was able to purchase the carving of an Inuit woman at work from a gallery in Yellowknife.

BACK ENDPAPER

The back endpaper features three favorite artifacts.

The painting of a duck landing was created by Louie, a kindergarten student at Pineridge Elementary in Kamloops, British Columbia. It is the most remarkable work of student art I have ever seen. Its true genius is the bird's right wing, which Louie imbued with a luminous rainbow. I traded a copy of *The Name of the Tree* for the painting, and when it was framed, I sent a photo of it to Louie with a note praising his extraordinary talent.

On the same trip I received a jolly handmade ceramic dinosaur posing with two stacks of my books — a thoughtful gift from the teachers and librarians attending the 1998 Sage Celebrations Children's Literature Conference.

As far back as I can recall, I wanted to own a Northwest Territories license plate due to its unique design. Who wouldn't? This one came as a gift straight off the recreation-room wall of its owner living in Fort Nelson, BC. I've never forgotten his generosity.

Turning the page, you will see that the curiosity cabinet and its contents are never far from my thoughts.

What would you put inside your curiosity cabinet to tell the story of your life?

Books mentioned:
Boy of the Deeps, written and illustrated by Ian Wallace. Groundwood Books, 1999.
Chin Chiang and the Dragon's Dance, written and illustrated by Ian Wallace. Groundwood Books, 1984.
The Mummer's Song, written by Bud Davidge, illustrated by Ian Wallace. Groundwood Books, 1993.
The Name of the Tree, written by Celia Barker Lottridge, illustrated by Ian Wallace. Groundwood Books, 1989.
The Sandwich, written and illustrated by Ian Wallace and Angela Wood. Kids Can Press, 1975.
The Sparrow's Song, written and illustrated by Ian Wallace. Groundwood Books, 1976.
Very Last First Time, written by Jan Andrews, illustrated by Ian Wallace. Groundwood Books, 1985.

Works that inspired the illustrations (in order of mention):
Owen Sound Public Library photo, courtesy of Willy Waterton, 1978.
Sparrow carving by Doug Robertson, 1986.
Tamarack geese, artists unknown, c. 1990.
Fishing-stage façade, artist unknown, c. 1995.
Mummers by Cara and Pam of Mummer's the Word, c. 2008 and c. 2013.
Innu Tea Doll, artist unknown, 1993.
O Canada lithograph by Joyce Wieland, 1970.
The Lost Salt Gift of Blood by Alistair MacLeod, 1976, used by permission of McClelland & Stewart, a division of Penguin Random House Canada Limited.
Painting by Marion Duncan, 1996.
Cabinet, artists unknown, c. 1995.
Paintings by Ted Harrison, courtesy of Wingate Arts Ltd.
Inuit sculpture by Jaco Ishulutaq, c. 1996.
Ceramic dinosaur by Doug Flach, 1998.